Like a Windy Day

FRANK ASCH & DEVIN ASCH

Voyager Books · Harcourt, Inc.

Orlando   Austin   New York   San Diego   London

For information about permission to reproduce selections from this book,
write to trade.permissions@hmhco.com or to Permissions, Houghton
Mifflin Harcourt Publishing Company, 3 Park Avenue,
19th Floor, New York, New York 10016.

www.hmhco.com

First Voyager Books edition 2008

Voyager Books is a trademark of Harcourt, Inc., registered in the
United States of America and/or other jurisdictions.

The Library of Congress has cataloged the hardcover edition as follows:
Asch, Frank.
Like a windy day/written and illustrated by Frank Asch and Devin Asch.
p.   cm.
Summary: A young girl discovers all the things the wind can do,
by playing and dancing along with it.
[1. Winds—Fiction.]   I. Asch, Devin.   II. Title.
PZ7.A778Lg 2002
[E]—dc21   2001005260
ISBN 978-0-15-216376-1
ISBN 978-0-15-206403-7 pb

SCP   18 17 16 15 14 13
4500816647

The illustrations in this book were drawn in pen and ink,
and colorized in Adobe Photoshop.
The display type was set in Zalderdash.
The text type was set in Goudy Old Style.
Color separations by Bright Arts Ltd., Hong Kong
Printed in China by RR Donnelley
Production supervision by Christine Witnik
Designed by Suzanne Fridley

To Eli and Tara

I want to play like a windy day.

I want to zoom down hillsides

and race through streets.

I want to scatter seeds,

turn windmills,

fly kites,

wave flags,

and snap wet sheets.

I want to play like a windy day.

I want to lift birds and butterflies in the sky.

I want to steal hats,

drive clouds and rain,

sail boats,

and make umbrellas fly!

I want to play like a windy day.

I want to shake the dew from a spider's web

and help her babies soar.

I want to blow through green grasses

and crash big blue waves on the shore.

I want to play like a windy day

and fly with the leaves from the trees.

I want to play like a windy day...

until I become like a gentle breeze.